STORY GROUND

THE ANTHOLOGY

STORY GROUND

THE ANTHOLOGY

edited by Paul Collis and Jen Crawford

RECENT WORK PRESS

Story Ground: The anthology
Recent Work Press
Canberra, Australia

Copyright © the authors, 2019

ISBN: 9780648685357 (paperback)

 A catalogue record for this book is available from the National Library of Australia

All rights reserved. This book is copyright. Except for private study, research, criticism or reviews as permitted under the Copyright Act, no part of this book may be reproduced, stored in a retrieval system, or transmitted in any form by any means without prior written permission. Enquiries should be addressed to the publisher.

Cover image by jade stephens on unsplash
Cover design: Recent Work Press
Set by Recent Work Press

recentworkpress.com

Australian Government
Indigenous Languages and Arts

UNIVERSITY OF CANBERRA

CENTRE FOR CREATIVE & CULTURAL RESEARCH
FACULTY OF ARTS & DESIGN

Contents

Introduction by Paul Collis ... 1

EMMA ADAMS
Baarka: Some thoughts on a women's place ... 5

WAYNE APPLEBEE
The Wayback Machine: Coniston at the event horizon ... 7
In the Shadows ... 8

KRIS BEATTIE
Writing off country about country:
Boudja Seeing Boudja ... 9

VALERIE M. BICHARD
Listening to Our Sea of Islands ... 10

PAUL COLLIS
Goin' Home ... 13
Hero Black, Remembered ... 14
Away Without Words ... 15

ELLIOT COOPER
Dirt as a physical action ... 16

JEN CRAWFORD
Stone river ... 18

DENNIS FOLEY
Ask why ... 20
Shadows ... 21
Precipitation ... 23

CHELLA GOLDWIN
Last Nations ... 24
The Protector's legacy ... 26

TJANARA GORENG GORENG
    They Whisper that Law   27
    Place   30
    People in my Street   32

BECCA GOSCH
    I'm not here   35
    Little Darling,   36
    Baakandji   37
    Ngemba   38

NYINGARI LITTLE
    Pearls   39
    Invisibility   40
    A warning   41
    Connection to Country   42

AZLAN MARTIN   43

HANGAMA OBAIDULLA
    The Apple   47

ROSITA RANDLE
    Two Gums Dancing in One Body   50

WENDY SOMERVILLE
    Swimming lesson   52
    I, we, the Aborigine   53
    Hey Trav   54
    After Cardboard Incarceration   55
    Mum all over   56
    Quandongs   57

ANDRAYA STAPP-GAUNT
    Rabbit-Girl   59

GEORGE VILLAFLOR
My country is here	60
The leader	63
Adaption	63
Goodbyes	63
Hope	63
Satisfaction	64
Culture	**64**

NOTES ON CONTRIBUTORS   65

Introduction

I want to acknowledge and thank the Ngunnawal people who have cared for and about their Country, and cared about their First Nations neighbours, the neighbours who are warmly remembered with each "Welcome to Country" that I've heard performed here in Canberra by Ngunnawal people. Thank you for making me feel welcome and for welcoming us all to your country.

I thank the Ngunnawal people for their generosity. I pay special respects to Aunty Agnes Shea, to Aunty Ros Brown and also to Mr. Richie Allan for all their guidance, support, respect and friendship toward me, and also for that same care and respect that they have shown toward all who have participated in the Story Ground Workshops and Story Ground Project. I don't think that Story Ground would have 'lived' without your welcome and support.

It is wonderful to be 'welcomed to country' by a Traditional Owner or Elder. For those who participated with me in the Story Ground Workshops, it was only after being welcomed in this way that we felt we could settle and write and create on Ngunnawal Country.

I came to Canberra from Newcastle in 2004 to complete a Bachelor's degree, which I'd begun at the University of Newcastle in 1995. I had completed two years of study at the Newcastle University before I returned to full-time work and had then not found time to complete my degree. In 2003 Newcastle University no longer offered the Bachelor Communication Degree that I'd begun back in 1995. Instead, I was offered opportunity to complete my degree in another faculty and subject area. But I was determined to finish the degree in the subject area that I'd begun with.

The University of Canberra offered a degree in Communications, and so I applied, and was accepted study. I began studying on Ngunnawal Country in the summer of 2004, and.have been studying here on Ngunnawal Country since.

In 2015 I had completed a creative PhD on an understanding/perspective of Barkindji Masculinity in the 21st century. I had written a creative novel as part of my thesis that helped explain the 'performances,' the psyche and cultures of some of my Country-men and women. My novel, *Dancing Home*, won the David Unaipon Award the next year.

These achievements had me in a bit of deep water, though, for some people began looking at me as an 'award winning author', who may be expected to know a bit about writing and literature. It's true, I had written the novel, butI didn't

1

know a great deal about creative writing. My academic subject area is mostly in Cultural Studies and in theories on communication – not in writing.I don't know all the rules that surround creative writing, and I had feelings of embarrassment whenever someone asked to speak with me about writing techniques, about plot, storyline and other such matters.

I met Assistant Professor Jennifer Crawford in 2016, in the staff tea room in Building 20. Jen was teaching Creative Writing in the Faculty Arts and Design at UC. My name had been suggested to her as 'someone' to speak with in relation to Creative Arts and Indigenous culture.

In Bourke, NSW, where I was born and lived during my primary years, out there on Barkindji country, I grew up listening to many of our older people in the community who were great storytellers. As Jen and I talked on, I told her that I'm more of a storyteller rather than a writer. And it was during this conversation in the tea room, three years ago, that Story Ground was 'born.'

Through funding which Jen Crawford and I were successful in winning via a Commonwealth Indigenous Languages and Arts (ILA) Program grant, a series of creative writing/making workshops were planned. We hoped to attract Aboriginal and Torres Strait peoples to come along, experience and share their creative story making, and declared the workshop open to all Aboriginal and Torres Strait peoples living in Canberra.

We are very grateful to the ILA program for making this work possible, and for supporting us in a range of connected activities. The ILA program, alongside the Centre for Creative and Cultural Research at UC, has helped an ever-growing network of story and creative making to thrive here.

A space was provided for Story Ground Workshopping on campus at UC and we hosted the first Story Ground workshop in January/February 2018. Three Story Ground workshops in all have been conducted over 2018 and 2019, alongside live readings, a symposium, and a number of other activities, cinlduing teaching and discussions of Story Ground pedagogy on campus to develop the presence of Indigenous Story in the university community.

Assistant Professor Jen Crawford was the power behind the establishing the funding of Story Ground. Grant applications are difficult to do, and winning a grant is a competitive act. Jen's persistence and skills not only completed the Commonwealth Indigenous Languages and Arts application, but helped to win the grant on which the whole Story Ground Project was built upon. And Jen is a wonderful teacher and mentor to me and to many. Her skill in the driving the workshops forward are testimony to her strengths as an academic and mentor.

Thank you, Jen, for all you have done, and for helping me every step of the way.

Award winning author and dear friend, Ms Lisa Fuller, co-hosted the second Workshop and wowed us with her vast knowledge of literature, editing and publishing. Lisa's engagement with us is like walking on sunshine – a sheer delight. Thank you, Lisa, you're a legend.

Professor Jen Webb has always been there to back us with Story Ground. Thank you, Jen, for your unending belief in all we were doing. And thank you for the great wisdom you have shown us all in helping us with getting Story Ground off the ground and into reality. You're a champion of the highest order.

Associate Professor Jordan Williams is a member of Story Ground team. Jordan's knowledge, strength, availability and advice are always there for Story Ground, and for me. Thank you, Jordan, for getting us there in the planning, and in the deed of making Story Ground a reality. Jordan's beautiful soup fed us during the second cold workshop, and still makes my lips hungry.... It is tastier and better than anything you'll buy in any shop. And I'll bet all of my pens on that! Thank you, Jordan, for everything...and, I mean for everything.

I also thank the wonderful Wendy Somerville, whose insights and ideas have given important direction at various times in the project. Your writing and sharing of ideas during the workshops and in the planning were quite remarkable Thank you to our hard working and good friend Becca Gosch. Becca's work as Project Officer has steered the ship beautifully, and her writing is sublimely crafted. A big thank you to the former member of 'The Shadows' basketball team, a friend and wonderful Brother, Kris Beattie. And an extra big thank you to that tall chap who knows a bit, *Einstein* (Wayne) Applebee, you've been good Brother and friend to the Story Ground project and workshops. Thanks Wayne.

Larry Brandy is a wonderful friend and Wiradjuri Story Teller and Performer. Thank you Brother Larry for sharing your stories and your culture with us. You are a wonderfully gifted artist. Your stories and support are greatly appreciated, and remembered by me, and by all of us.

Without the help and friendships of all of you mentioned above the workshops would never have got off the ground. You were there in the beginning, arranging tables, setting up, carrying food, directing people to the rooms. And then you participated in the workshops as writers and artists. And you were there at the end of the day too, when the packing up needed to be done. I truly mean it when I say I could not have done this without you. Your friendships and help mean so much to me.

In Barkindji and Kunya culture, I was taught that it is a very 'bad thing' to ever leave anyone out. Our customs are sharing cultures. And so too with Story Ground. Many non-Aboriginal and Torres Strait peoples showed us support and encouragement. And a number of non-Aboriginal and Torres Strait people were welcomed into Story Ground as artists, writers and storytellers. This mixture of art is a blessing to both see, read and experience. Thank you one and all for your gifts and work.

There are way too many writers and artists to mention in detail here. Some of you dropped into the workshops, stayed a while then moved on; others stayed the whole nine yards. But you are all what made Story Ground—your writings, and stories, your attentiveness and support to each is the heart of Story Ground. You've held stories safely and dearly. Your willingness to share, and your bravery are the very foundation of Community and Culture. I'm so proud to have met you all, and for you taking me into your worlds through Story Ground.

*

The Story Ground Anthology is a combination of prose writing, poetry and storytelling. The authors come from far flung places. Their writings here are breathtakingly powerful. This anthology is for the keeping, I believe, and for returning to—a collection that you will find yourself reading and embracing, time and again.

I thank everyone who participated with Story Ground—you've helped change my life course with your work. I congratulate all the writers, storytellers and artists whose works appear here in this edition. Well done. And thank you.

Story Ground: The anthology is dedicated to our dear Brother Thomas Subasio, a leader who held his stories and his people sacred. A wonderful man and friend to Story Ground.

It is also dedicated to author, activist and true brave-heart, Kerry Reed-Gilbert. A brilliant writer and activist, herself, Kerry was also a patient and wonderful Sista. Kerry was always happy to read a poem or piece of my writing, I really love and appreciate all you did for me/us, Kerry. The Cherry Picker's daughter now lays in Ngunnawal soil, and in the hearts of those who of us who knew her. Kerry's writings are read throughout the world. You're the very finest example of strength and art, Kerry

—Dr. Paul Collis

Emma Adams

Baarka: Some thoughts on a women's place

At the end of 2018, I travelled with other writers and poets associated with the University of Canberra to Bourke and Brewarrina. The agenda was to be acquainted with these places, their rich history and culture, and to write.

All of us women were getting a sense of each other, sussing each other out. The elder Baarkinji women who were our hosts didn't say much. They were scanning the road for roos and emus who had a tendency to dart across at the last minute, although the quietness could also have been a few nerves as our city-built minivan skidded across the bulldust or lurched and groaned as we hit a big rock.

On arrival, somehow our hosts seemed more nimble than when we pulled ourselves into the minivan earlier this morning. There is being on country, and being in *special places* on country. This was a special women's place. There was a girlish energy, and a scramble to arrange tea and cheese and bickies where everyone pitched in chatting and laughing.

Coolibah trees sheltered us from the harsh sun. Behind us, vast ochre-coloured floodplains stretched out to a horizon dotted with trees. The river was not visible in front of us because of its steep banks but as it snaked around in the distance we could see a shine of water between some outcrops of black rocks.

The river's name is Baarka, which my friend Paul tells me means 'darling', loved one. This one word embeds connection and love. Baarka is not a human or a plant or an animal, but it is a force of life. Our rivers come from sacred places, from the tops of mountains, sides of gullies, fed from tropical storms in the north or they emerge from underground aquifers. Rivers are our lifeblood, and are paths that connect us. Abundance.

We sat longer, drank more tea, grazed on the food, some of us had a smoke and we listened. Stories about this river and growing up in Bourke. As the afternoon edged on and the others became quieter in their own thoughts I took a look around.

This wasn't my country, and I knew I had to be careful, meaning respectful. I was a guest here and didn't want to venture where I wasn't supposed to be so I used my caution walking along the river bank. Some places communicate, give us a sense of recognition or feelings, and sometimes, they communicate a threat, where you just shouldn't be. In the past, I've had this feeling in the base of my stomach, and the back of my neck and throat, and I've learned—sometimes the hard way—to take notice.

I didn't get the harsh warning. Instead, a beautiful sense of comfort and excited happiness welled up inside me. I'm guessing it was a leak of oxytocin, that wonderful hormone that is involved in attachment, birth and mothers' milk. This was a women's place, this was a mother's place. It was a natural depression alongside the riverbank flanked by trees whose rough outstretched limbs skimmed a meter or so from the ground. A place of shade and soft earth a few steps away from where the water's edge would normally be. Down further was a rock formation that I couldn't help but think looked very much like fish traps, similar to the most famous ones which were only a day or so walk away in Brewarrina. Good for a feed of fish for the woman and her attendants.

I imagined a scene. A circle of women helping each other, the river Baarka providing relief and nourishment and a fire scenting the air. Babies born and nestled against their mothers. The intensity of childbirth, border between life and death. Generation after generation over thousands and thousands of years. How many babies were born here? What beautiful stories were created on this river side? This was a sacred place. Baarka, the ultimate midwife and mother.

Let's think of something else—it might sound crude but I'm angry. Imagine if a white explorer had birthed a turd here: there would have been a plaque. There's no marker, no sign so people visiting here would not know its significance.

Because of the nation's ignorance, we have allowed this river, the bloodstream of the people here, the Baarkinji and further along, the Ngemba and many other mobs, to be cut off. What happens if you tie off someone's bloodstream?

Standing on the edge of the river, where it would have naturally spread out as it snaked along, the old trees, including some huge old river gums, looked tortured. They are balanced on a network of exposed spindly roots, the life giving soil having been gradually eroded away. The regular floods that are needed to replenish the land do not happen anymore. The greedy dams have taken the water, weirs have been built blocking the natural flow, and introduced carp thud against its banks. Even much of the thirty thousand year old fish traps were blown up with dynamite for a ferry that operated very briefly. The river has been abused then ignored. Today, this river is shrunken, sluggish and malodorous.

Baarka is the Darling river and our darling is in her death throes.

Wayne Applebee

The Wayback Machine: Coniston at the event horizon

Between the dreaming and reality, steam accompanies each breath, dim the light —fingers cold these drivers of the Wayback Machine. Transposed to another time and place, a journey of the mind.

The sun is high in the forenoon; on the horizon shimmers eight, maybe ten, blue tops, that meld with their horses. Realisation grips, panic fear and foreboding, they are known. Those able turn to run. Some are swift, others can only do their best.

We are at the event horizon. Mothers desperate, children hold tight, babies cry—their reconciliation with Baiame is nigh.

The pounding of hooves an assault on the senses, taste and smell. Horses froth and heave saliva, a lather of sweat where the rider once sat. Attentions are focussed by a tree. He relieves himself—dusty uniform, leather-clad, the piss falls raising dust.

Finished, he then pulls a blackened corn cob pipe from a vest pocket. With it settled in the palm of his hand he holds he looks about and musses a while with the index finger, stuffing it full. With a practised hand he fires a match and a waft of smoke fills his lungs. A captured audience impaled, no chance of escape, they watch transfixed in deathly anticipation, never daring to move.

He draws his heavy revolver from its leather pouch. The first shot renders the air, followed closely by a cacophony of shot.

No sound; but silence— a baby crawls to its mother, arm outstretched, fingers spread, it paws at the breasts of its life-giver. A rivulet of red covers the bare breast. Streaks of brown appear against the crimson where the baby's fingers seek attention from a prone body. All around it is still, except for a swirl of dust where the now-departed horses tilled the soil. At a distance now, the horses are disappearing against the horizon from whence they had come. A shimmer, and they are gone. A baby cries.

"No, your honour, what is the use of a wounded blackfellow hundreds of miles from civilization?" asserts Constable Murray.

In the Shadows

Peering out the window, dark clouds about.
Beyond the towering walls, mountains covered white.
The clock below the church steeple says eight thirty.
The bell sounds as each section's lights go out: One Two and Three.
The bell sounds as the radio comes on, each section's lights go on: One Two and Three.
The clock below the church steeple says eight thirty.
Peering out the window there is blue, but no light reaches here.
What day is it?
'Eight thirty.'

Kris Beattie

Writing off country about country:
Boudja Seeing Boudja

A diasporic Noongar on Ngunnawal boudja
watches a rising sun bring life to light on the east,
lush, green mountains that overlook and protect Ngunnawal boudja.
Ngunnawal boudja's winter is freezing cold—
once you would've needed a yonga bwoka to keep warm,
but now young fellas wear hoodies and jackets.
Noongar boudja is hot—no hoodies or jackets needed back home.
Summertime is tip-toe-hot-sand-dancing time, on Noongar boudja.
Balayi!!! Watch out for woggle (his bite can kill).

Valerie M. Bichard

Listening to Our Sea of Islands

> *Oceania is vast. Oceania is expanding, Oceania is hospitable and generous, Oceania is humanity rising from the depths of brine and regions of fire deeper still, Oceania is us. We are the sea, we are the ocean, we must wake up to this ancient truth and together use it to overturn all hegemonic views that aim ultimately to confine us again, physically and psychologically, in the tiny spaces that we have resisted accepting as our sole appointed places and from which we have recently liberated ourselves. We must not allow anyone to belittle us again, and take away our freedom.*

Epeli Hau'ofa, "Our Sea of Islands" (2008, 39)

R-1-3-1-9-5-9 Miss Valerie Mary Tinai – Height 3ft 2 inches. I'm searching an old passport for a clue, a clue that could hint at destiny, a clue to understand an expanding Oceania. I wonder whether the answer can be found in the face of a child too young to sign her own name? The passport reads that I am joining my mother. Embossed with the crest of the New Zealand Department of Internal Affairs, the black and white photograph of my three year old self evokes a soft pastel blue dress with white buttons, collar and trim. Parnell, where our house in Ruskin Street still stands, postman's knock, a small creek with apple trees and watermelon, a walk up a steep hill to a rose garden, naughty cat, bread and cheese. Deeper still lies the pain of my ancestors as they are branded with hot irons, chained and forced on slave ships across the Atlantic ocean. Whispering voices chant an ancient language now lost. The pulsating rhythm of the chant is there to keep me focused on the horizon that separates the land of the living from the land of our ancestors. If these memories can be evoked by a photograph and mingle with the present, is it also possible to reveal a life journey in the eyes of a child? There was a time when I could not only see, I could feel, smell and taste precious memories of happiness, fear, excited anticipation or deep dark sorrow. Now the details of the journey that brought me here are slowly fading. The motivation for our migration is tainted by the hope and expectations, found, in the dreams of the living and lost in those since past. So frozen in an eternal present, this small piece of evidence without ancestral memory becomes fixed into dominant migration narratives. What does an expanding Oceania mean without our ancestral knowing? The first wave after the White Australia Policy, British subject and New Zealand citizen, eyes black, hair black...

Looking out through a wooden window frame onto the deck of the ship that carried me from New Zealand to Sydney's circular quay, I notice something puzzling. In the ship's background, set against a blanket of grey sky there is a dark mass that moves like a morphing mountain range. The rigid white parallel lines of the ship's railings move up and down, up and down ... each time the ship rises it reaches a point where it starts to fall, then lurches itself forward before coming down with an explosive white spray that fans into the sky and across the deck. The artificial horizon looks hard, determined and uncompromising, without seeming to breach the deck, or as I now remember it, the moving mountain and sky seem to have a spatial dimension of their own. The mountain range shifts and becomes a giant tilting plain that stretches off into the distance creating its own diagonal horizon, and the flat surface heaves as though it is taking a few long, deep well-deserved breaths.

In this moment of respite a beam of light pierces the grey, in search of something unknown. It illuminates unseen detail and colour across each surface it touches. It crosses the deck and disappears as the distance between the liquid horizon shrinks and a huge mountain rises higher than the railing, almost swallowing the sky. Suddenly, it drops out of sight, leaving the boat suspended against the flat grey wall, pitching towards, then away, from left to right. As quickly as it disappeared, the rolling mountain range returns. I start to cry. I don't cry because I feel sick or afraid, I don't sense fear. I'm returning to a dream—but wait, I'm no longer dreaming. The mountain is moving and alive. I am alive and moving and that artificial horizon is the only thing that separates me from my ancestral memory... still beneath the surface of a flowing river, speckled light ripples over pebbles that stare into the boundless sky. A bamboo raft glides on rapids towards an evening meal by hurricane light. Assisted by a sturdy pole and the movement of her agile feet, Bubu easily finds her balance to the sound of splashing, squeaking, rolling bamboo. A baby wrapped snugly on her back memorizes the rhythm of the pebbled river and her grandmother's heartbeat. Along with the smell of smoky wood fire and coconut oil on her Bubu's ebony skin the child senses the majestic presence of the surrounding mountains. Strong hands guide the craft with skill and grace past laughing children who call out the baby's name over the sound of rushing water. The children swim against the strong current with enthusiasm then randomly, one by one they relinquish themselves to the movement of water. They bob up and down, swiftly passing the raft. Beyond the rapids, embraced by deep swirling water, their laughter is gently silenced. At the same time the bamboo craft comes to rest upon the shore.

Paul Collis

Goin' Home

'How we git to Redfern?' he asks.
'I'll show ya, Brother.'

Hail a cab, off to the other world we sail. Me and the four of them,
through city traffic laughing, pointing at things.
They speak in language I don't know.
David does his best to interpret. Whether he is telling me the truth, only they know.
He is happy. Can't wait to get there,
to be out of the light and into the black.
On the Block, a crowd comes a-runnin' to get a close look.
Beside the railway fence, next to other Brothers, we make a place to drink.
The beer gets drunk. So do we. We settle into conversation, and the crowd thins away.
Green weed blows blue smoke, crooks and kickers drift 'round.
Cool dudes drive past in flash cars, looking us up and down.
Others, less fortunate, hobble past in crooked style.
Some offer a sly smile as they hurry away to the Lane—where the gear is.
Cops drive past too, on another street.
Everybody breathes easier seeing the back end of their taillights as they drive on to Newtown.

Sun-cast shadows hang over city buildings; the weather changes.
David and his Brothers speak to each other using body language—
shift the hip, bow the shoulder, blink an eye.
I know this language.
Wondering, 'What next? –Stay here and drink; or look for more yarndi?'
I lean towards him and softly say, 'Brother. I gotta go. Want anything? Or… you want me to take you back?'
Glassy-eyed, he looks into the fire.
'We right Brother. Thank you. Take care, hey?' he says, as if talking to the flames.

Hero Black, Remembered

Baiame changed shape at night.
One became two –Two Snakes – The Rainbow.
One Snake, Guldabira, danced North.
The other, Wartanuring, danced South – down Menindee way.
Rainbow Snakes made the rivers. Made them join, in love.
Guldabira moved then, towards Wanaaring, leaving water stones and ochre.
After the rivers joined the Rainbow Snakes became One again.
Baiame left the skins' remnants on earth, and then returned to the sky.
Water stones bring water, ochre paint bring spirits into the body.
My River – Barka, she's empty now. But I know where the water stones are
I'll paint-up in ochre and crush mica to add, to make my black skin shine,
I'll dance and Baiame will see me.

Away Without Words

From sleep into the Dreaming you slipped through in shadowed morning, silently.
No word of goodbye was offered as the then became the Great Forever.
In moonlit trees, the messenger's birds cried for you, as they sang your song.
I knew they were telling me 'someone is gone'; but I didn't imagine who.
Through my window, a shadow passed with no form.
And, in the sun morning, in the stillness, came the message, this time by telephone.
I know now that the passing was you.

Elliot Cooper

Dirt as a physical action

Run.
I cannot think of anything worth saying more.

Run until you are dirt tired.
Spend energy.
Make yourself poor.
What problem solves industry,
Not created by productivity?
Run.

Fall and scrape
Open the skin
Drip blood on the earth
What kindness
I am dirt.

Exhale expend excrete exhaust.
Leave it all out there.
Become the earth.
All *things* come from people who fail to make themselves tired.

Energy unused goes to industry and erecting.
    And a concrete slab to mount it on.
Constructing better garbage more environmentally: Environmentalling.
Engineering to sustain unsustainable lives more sustainably: We are in the
    Sustainathon.

Left over energy. What did roughness and slowness ever do that you hurt
    them so forcefully?

Run: sweat drenched, dirt tired, at a high point in Country.

I sit on the earth and say "woot!" in satisfaction.
Ants splay in veins over my ochre-smothered limbs.
In this place is air, and peace, and dirt as a physical action.

Dirt tired without a negative thought in mind
I recall what Owen the poet said to me,
"There's nothing I miss about electricity."

Jen Crawford

Stone river

I was doing the dishes looking out the window into the night and wondering whether these two groups of kids in the park were about to start fighting and then they turned towards the cottage, towards me, and their shouts grew rhythmical, and louder. and then I realized that I was peering at them, that through the broken blind they could see me peering at them, and that the meaning of the hole in the window above Paul's head was a stone, and that the meaning of the cage around the cottage was a stone too. I stepped away from the sink and went into the lounge, where Paul was hunched under a blanket, listening, and I went in there as though excited or seeking an explanation.

-

after we picked up the rubbish around the river my father's back was aching, and when my son woke in the night with a sore stomach I began to be afraid, thinking of the dirty nappy I'd seen but not touched in the hollow of a rock. I am a rubbish pick-upper, Theo said. We are going to Japan but we are not Japanese. in the morning he was well, and in the late afternoon I walked back along the Ngunnhu through warm stripes of light and shade. where the pelicans had lifted together to wheel across the whole bed, here a single egret, and then a single pelican circled low, attendant to a point. ears. there's a kangaroo in the river, alive and alone among the weeds.

-

in Bourke I drive through a give way without slowing and then I end up on the wrong side of the road. my father drives through a give way without slowing. my husband, driving, ends up on the wrong side of the road. at Toorale Station the wind gives a most gentle welcome, and then it strengthens, insistent, entirely steady.

-

I like the work it's not as angry as I expected. Brewarrina to Narromine corpses and loose cotton. swathes of large trees uprooted by flood. I like autumn leaves. empty fields stacked with white bales, dry creeks, dry rivers.

lone roos, small emus alone or in pairs, high fences, fur and bones. what you see is a stone smash in the window. I like sparkling water slipping down over the weir. there's so much potential there. we can clean up the point of view. the car could be damaged. I don't know why I saw it up ahead I didn't swerve. it's about the technique. our roadkill too fat to drive over.

-

what are we going to pull some bags out. out of the water that's living the rocks. fast in slow. are we going to be hands in there or what. whether it's moving. don't know the smell. don't know if we're sick. crusts on the rock. white, bright green. slow hairskins. letting out or letting in. part of an animal or water. on its whole way around. and whether we feel that that is moving. the rock, here, and the water that comes back

kind of time. like an animal is thirsty and will drink. to say, evaporation is not waste. all the way aroundthe vast until same water same rock a kiss oh hardly moved. so what are we going to dig cans out. get cut. to one side or another of a skin. dig how far down the drying mud. to more. to where we feel better or sick. like what's alive. like anyone who makes their home in a can. and anyone who lives in plastic bags. being disturbed. feeling cast. and what are we going to go home. step outside of anger, the sun. date some carbon. put a finger on it, what we're being told. come back. hardly move. and put hands in

into glue. fish banked dead beneath the weir. stones smashed to mud. let's go, say it. get washed. say, I've got an answer and it's ornamental. we slip our pond. we're gasping. we thrive. take five minutes and run the river backwards. spend a long time on this aesthetic and watch out it's not finished. lock your river. hold close the stones. we're casting

rosy children to dive and swim, fair girls' feet in the rippling brim. floating parts   in contagious velocity. and sucking the air, rank and sweet, nitroglycerin.

Dennis Foley

Ask why

Ask why
Said the child
Ask why
Asked the youth
Ask why
Stated the adult.
Don't know,
Always wrong
Cause I am just a Koori male.
Typical poor blackfella me
Said the spouse
From her unprivileged youth
For her standpoint was worse than mine
In some ways.
Yet;
She sees a glass half full.
Whereas the Koori only gets
A glass half empty.
Ask why?
I just do not know!
I just do not know....

Shadows

The shadows in the family
The anthropologist and sociologist
Haunted my grandparents
And now me.
Black Shadows
Preaching negative discourse
On my children
Stereotypes that are self-fulfilling
So they thought!

Good teachers often turned into cultural auditors
In my children's struggle for an education
My daughter was strong
She hid beneath the sheet of the shadow
Kept a low profile
And quietly achieved
Until she won
Two degrees and three daughters
All in the sun.
My son attacked,
Always questioning
Always trying to paint black as white
Creating anger
Confusion
And ultimately self-doubt.
Alcohol was an early crutch
Then ice was the medium
That hides the shadows
Or does it empower them?

So many talents
Lives and hopes
Slide into the sludge of colonialism
A dark place
So cold and evil

Where lateral violence and trauma is the norm.
Child against parent
And the anthropologist laughs
As they close their book
A black book called I told you so!

Precipitation

Rain,
cleaning drains
washing leaves on journeys
into holes
deep deep holes
no return
and dust
sweetened
rusty iron left shimmering
drops now brown
stain the ground.

And life begins!

Chella Goldwin

Last Nations

The First Nations were the first here
not the second or the third.
Everyone knows
first in best dressed.
Being first Nations
does that mean no one was here
before them?
The place was empty
terra nullius?
No man's land.
What if the place wasn't empty
before them?
What if the land was full of people
the whole time?
I wonder if anyone thought of that?
This would mean
that they probably weren't
the First Nations.
First Nations would be
the first to arrive.
But what if they didn't arrive?
That would mean they weren't first.
If you look at it from a particular angle
or any angle really.
If you look at it from the north
from the south
from the east
from the west
even looking at it from the middle
it's still the same angle.
They were always here

from the beginning.
But they weren't first.
I wonder who made up that lie
that they were first.
The First Nations.
They originated here.
The original nations.
The owners.
They were always here.
Always will be.
But now they are last.
The last nations.
Everlasting.

The Protector's legacy

My father told me
he lived under the rule of a despised
white Protector.
He ran the reserves
on the Torres Strait Islands
and Cape York Peninsula.
The Protector's black face is found
all throughout those areas.
...this is his legacy.

Tjanara Goreng Goreng

They Whisper that Law

Land...
whispering
stories
Ancestors past
Raining 'cross country
Sharing
Caring
Knowing
Calling... to my Soul
Kurunpa
Tjukurpa
Baiame
Pulka

Stories come
From long ago...
Wandering
long dreaming tracks
Smoothed over by
Bullock tracks
Mala gone...
Meat for dogs now
Sheep...no use
Just woolly coat
Not like possum...
Eat 'em good
That porcupine...
Nice earrings too...

Modern dancer now
Blakfella I am

Story come
Story shared
They whisper
'cross time
Don't forget
Say them
Old ones....
Don't forget us
You
Them...
Stories whispered
Songs sung

Vibrate that corroboree
Dance...
under my feet
Sun streams
Rainbows
Down my cheeks
Bless my heart
Bless my life
They give me
Joy
Love
In the pain
Longing...
Always
Longing....

Never leave me
Them old ones
Even
When I leave them
They come
Don't want me forget
That business
That tjukurpa

That kurunpa
That Baiame
That Law

Place

The red earth stretches in front of me miles unending beckoning me urging me to move into and beyond it I want it to enable an escape from what's behind me

My mind turns to remembering why I want to run into that red desert
The scream remains silent inside. He comes in the night. Never to rest but to inflict pain
A child feels that whip of the hand on the head waking suddenly.....why?
Again and again until I silently fall asleep sobbing inside

Night again and I wait in fear never to be released.....
Even my mother my brothers and sisters cannot save me as they sleep silently on the verandahs of our wind-blown Queenslander

Sometimes I imagine when I'm swimming in the pool early in the morning before school that I could drown....Then it would end
But what good would that do
That'd just finish me and then I'd miss out on a life....

It'll pass I tell myself, one day I'll be gone and one day I'll be free but the feeling never leaves me of wanting to run into that red desert and never come back
No matter what awaits me it would be less painful than this I tell myself
The naivete of a child not knowing what could be out there just wanting to make sure I never feel this again....

Western Queensland full of bull riders and cowboys, the racists alongside woolly sheep and stinking cattle reminding me of the trap I'm in
White girls with blond ponytails, air-conditioned houses and nice straight cleanly mowed front lawns
Mothers that dress in the latest 1950's fashion and drive Holden cars to church on Sunday kneeling sweetly before the priest for redemption and holy communion

It's only I who feels outside this place, not dressed nor blessed

Wondering if they can all tell what's behind the facade of black skin and white lies

The polka dot dress and white patent shoes supposed to make me feel like I belong

But inside is the feeling of never... and the red earth wind beckons calling voices on the wind and it would be over... buried there happy again

People in my Street

People in my street
Always walk down the middle of the street
no car
Walking down the middle line
Always blacks
Aboriginal mob
Walking down
that centre line
Like they need to see
Left and right
See it all
To be safe
Not sure
Why

There he goes
Blak man
With his child
On his shoulder
Little girl
Ponytail
Pink top
Nice Nikes
Deadly pants
Crisp white shirt
Baseball cap on straight
She laughing
Loving her dad

There she goes
Blak woman
Long black hair
Big sunglasses
White baseball cap

On straight
Dressed to the nines
Tight black jeans
Sparkly leather jacket
Nice big
black tote bag
Carrying her luggage
On her way
Where....

Next police car
White
Big pink and blue stripes
Loud
Make sure we know
It's them....
Slowly rolling
Down the street
Silent menace
Looking in all the houses
As they go
Making sure
We being
Straight
Good
Blakfellas

Neighbour
White woman
Cross the street
White woman
Neighbour
Next door
Proper good
White woman
Neighbour
Banging on her fence

Frustrated
The dog broke it
This morning
They never walk
Down that centre line

Then he walked back
That blak man
Up the street
Centre line
Daughter on his shoulders
Going home
He lives two doors down
Never seen her before
She's new...
Visiting...
The neighbours
Two doors down

Police man
Drive down that centre line
Again
Seeing me
Through my window
Now white man
Walking
On my grass
Not on the centre line
????
Why doesn't anyone
Walk on the left or the right
Why do police man
Drive up the centre
That normal street
No sign says
Walk
Drive
Down the middle!

Becca Gosch

I'm not here

What do you
Do when you
Aren't there?
I stand
Barefooted
On bitumen
That burns.
Let it do what
Nothing else can.
Burn out the
Desperate need
For these feet
To walk past,
The present.
They're burning.
Good.

Little Darling,

Do you remember when you thought
The meat-eater was coming to get you?
                                    You feared it and revered it.
Not just the meat-eater.
The plant-eaters, land-walkers, sea-dwellers,
High-fliers & sky-gliders too.
Fear didn't bother you so blown away you were
By the strange beauty of those giants.
                                    They were larger than life; then

My love,

I long for them to roam the earth
Again, to step out of my imagination,
Out of history and make real for me
                                    Something larger. Not larger than life.

Just larger than the
Man-shaped meat-eater
Who got you?
All those years ago.

Love,
        Why're you crying?

Oh Nan,
        I've burnt my feet.

Baakandji

If all you see
Is land and sky
Well, we're different
You and I.
Feel come to life
All creatures
That call you,
Home.
Listen out for
Just one

I'll be the land and
You be the sky
Are we still different
You and I

Ngemba

Last night all words were
Laid to rest among the stars.
Us too.

This evening the sky
Set fire to their remains.
Ours too.

Morning brings our ashes home,
Our stories home.
Us too.

Dust now, we must choose
Rise or settle.
We Rise.

Nyingari Little

Pearls

Tears drop like pearls
On a string necklace
Expensive and pretty
But the fakes are glass
And their shards are sharp

Invisibility

Invisibility
Is a curse
Not a power
Loneliness is
Being in a room where
Everyone knows each other
But for some reason
No one can remember your name
Were you there?
I don't remember
A member of the living
Among a world of ghosts.

A warning

Be careful not to sit too still
Not to listen too carefully
Or breathe so deep
Because the emptiness
Will pull and pluck and tug
On your poor and heavy heart

Connection to Country

We've always known: healthy country, healthy people. We're happier on country, healthier on country. But no one believed us until Western Science proved it. My friend—white, she is—once asked me 'What's the difference between here or there? Why does it matter? It's all just dirt." Of course, she wouldn't understand—all her ancestors have ever known is conquer, profit, conquer, profit. Never return. Safe to say we aren't friends anymore.

Connection to country is a concept few may ever understand. It's a feeling and therefore a knowing. It's a length of rubber band with one end wrapped around your heart; your soul, and the other end attached to the land. There is no tension when you're on country—no stress, just deep breaths of fresh air after only ever tasting smoke. But that tension will come if you stray too far. You will lose yourself. How can you live when that rubber band is stretched beyond capacity? How can your heart beat freely? You must snap back home as quick as you can before you go too far and lose that connection forever.

Azlan Martin

my mother dissects the past into segments

peels layers of rind
from her flesh

flavours the citrus
with myrtle, ginger and cardamom
dry from summer heat and drought

my mother passes me a plate

begins our story from the conclusion
and orange rind falls to the garden soil
with the cadence of her voice

my mother spins tales
of eucalypt and honeycomb
weaving our past into something palatable

flowers will bloom in spring

this is what it feels
to bury my mother with words
this is what it feels
to build my mother whole again
this is what it feels
to throw out the whole rotten fruit
and plant the seed

this is me painting our future
of memories
and calling it spring

because women in my family
build homes from our skin
stitched from sandcastles

before we are washed away

it is a special
kind of violence for the heart
to lose the tongue

un-stitch your teeth girl
the salt is calling your name
come, un-bind your voice

oh, astronaut sky
dreaming with soft winter grey:
let the storm take you

you are coming together in waves, learning to swim as you lose sight of shore.

take one apple
seed, plant deep
in mother's earth

succour life with the bone
of your ancestors
feed with blood of your history

careful not to overwater
with salted tears

for fear the fruit will turn sour.

Hangama Obaidulla

The Apple

Soraya looked around her room. It was quite a small room with a low ceiling, a dark green curtain which was patched with black pieces hanging on the wall in front of the small window that blocked the sunlight, making the room darker. She could not forget the memory of the young boy, who pulled his bike right in front of her and then turned around. He hit her on the back with an empty plastic bottle; she had never seen him before.

Lost in thoughts, she reached for the white scarf. While she was covering her head and shoulders, she thought of an idea; to cover her face so that no one could recognise her. She grabbed her bag and her shoes from the cupboard. As she was leaving the house, she saw an poor old man carrying a child. The child looked quite sick and she was screaming loudly, begging her father not to take her to the hospital. The old man looked extremely tired. As he was putting her on the back of his bicycle, he kissed her, calming her down. It was a busy morning; the neighbours were talking; people were coming and going, Soraya was not aware of what was going on. The next-door neighbour was from a very rich family; they had moved to Kabul recently and they were busy preparing a bridal party. A miserable young man was busy delivering fruit boxes. Another young man came out from the same house; he grabbed two apples from the box, he put one apple into his jacket left-hand pocket. He had a bite of the other apple and threw the other half away as he jumped on his bike.

Soraya entered a long empty road. It was a hot sunny day. The young man had had her under surveillance since she'd left home. He'd parked his bike and was walking closely behind her. She'd heard a strange noise so she turned back to see who it was. It was the same guy. She felt dismayed and dreadfully nervous. She put her head down and began walking faster and faster.

Halfway down to the road, she stopped walking because her old worn sandals were uncomfortable. She heard his footsteps very clearly and she made herself busy to avoid him and reacted as if a small piece of gravel was hurting her foot. She felt uncomfortable and worried. He came to the corner of the road and tried to catch her surreptitiously.

He leaned himself on the wall and stood up right in front of her. Soraya quickly looked around. There was no one except him in the long empty road far from her home. He had a smile on his face, and looked at her with his bloodshot eyes, 'You walk from here every day, without a male,' he said, while he was scratching his neck. He moved in a different manner to express his strength. She didn't like the look of him.

Instead of leaving he moved closer. He said to her, 'Look - something I want to tell you,' and he pulled out an apple from his left-hand jacket pocket. He took a dirty handkerchief from around his neck to clean the apple; he grabbed her hand and placed the apple into her hand. 'I don't need it,' she said. Her face flushed red, a warm sweat was running from the top of her head down to her feet. She couldn't walk, or look around; she felt insulted, she wanted to shout. He pushed her. He put his feet on top of her feet and pressed hard and stopped her from moving.

Both her eyes opened very wide and wider still, her upper lip shivered. Tears were dropping from the corner of her eyes. 'You know what? I don't like to see your crazy reaction. I just want to say, I love you very much,' he said with an unpleasant and violent voice. That's why I am here.'

When he stepped back, Soraya saw he had a gun at the right-side of his waist. She felt all her body burning and the energy drained from her. Her heart was pumping wildly and she could sense a strange noise around her.

Soraya looked at the apple. 'It's ridiculous,' she said angrily. 'I will not throw it away, I could offer it to a beggar, maybe.' Then she put the apple into her bag. After he left, she was felt very disturbed and unable to move. Her toes were bleeding. She held her breath and her eyes followed him to the end of the road until he disappeared.

Soraya understood very clearly that it was sexual harassment, and she had been abused by a young man. It was definitely not a proposal.

'He didn't look like an educated, smart guy, because they won't express their good feelings with violence or unpleasantness,' she said to herself very loudly. She had only one pair of black shoes which she had bought from a second-hand shop, and she wore them to school daily. Her shoes were damaged and so she thought that she should take them to the cobbler to be repaired. Soraya struggled to walk to the shoemaker's shop. When she reached the main street she heard a faint sound. She saw an old man sitting on the corner of the street and busy working on a piece of cobbling. She asked him to repair her shoes. He turned around, and she saw that he was that same old man she'd seen carrying the child that morning.

Soraya was happy that her shoe was fixed. When he asked her to pay for the repair, she said, 'I don't have even a small amount to pay you, I'm sorry, but I can give you something rather than money.'

'What is it?' The old man asked with little hope.

Soraya grabbed the apple from her bag and gave to the shoemaker. 'Oh, an apple, thank you," he said with a big smile on his face.

Rosita Randle

Two Gums Dancing in One Body

I am a stranger,
        but I feel home
I am a stranger here but plants are like family
Like a child, telling a story from a book whose words I can't read, whose pictures are a gateway.

Welcomed by the kindness of those who've not been shown it
Feeling like I've been given a key
Feeling like I've been given a moment
A thought
A breath
A story

I feel the rain like a heartbeat
Water sounds like childhood
Deeply
Here the air is different.
Deeply
I am different

A motif of two tears at my story
You told me Canberra heals us
I looked to see I was bleeding
This isn't my country
But
It is my heart
This isn't my history
but two gums dance in one body

My hips carry the ache of a thousand mothers,
But I bore her in my heart and grew her there.

A thousand stitches in a line but I can't follow straight
A thousand ways we're the same
      Or so you told me.
But my mother is the trees.

Wendy Somerville

Swimming lesson

I want to swim like the big kids, their bodies slithering through the muddy water like snakes through the long grass. One minute seen, the next minute hidden. The big ones dive and sometimes belly flop. I can belly flop, but it hurts. I want to join in. Walking in the shallow part and playing on the edges is what the little ones do. I want to be a big girl and swim out to the drums and dive off like the big kids. I sook because I am stuck here with squishy mud creeping between my toes. Am I going to end up cemented in this spot without ever growing up?

I ask that person, that person who should be a grown up. 'Dad, can you teach me to swim?'

He laughs and picks me up, 'C'mon, I'll teach you.'

He carries me into the middle of the Old Res and throws me. 'Now swim.'

I sink and panic because all I see is brown water. I am suffocating and need to get back up. My hands start waving, pulling against the water until my eyes see all that surrounds me. I take a breath and start to sink, only to pull against the water to get up out of this murky, brown and scary place. I think I see a crocodile and push my arms so hard that they hurt. I break the surface and see the bastard laughing, yelling 'swim to me.' I want to get at him, tell him I hate his guts. I know that he will never get it. I manage to stay afloat and windmill my arms and kick my legs towards him. He moves backwards and eventually I can stand. I cry, he laughs. 'Look who can swim,' he says. I still can't swim properly, just enough to save myself.

I, we, the Aborigine

We sat around his table playing canasta and talking. Not him but us. We talked about being Koori. I don't recall what all we said, maybe one sister said she didn't like being in a crowd of blackfullas – why wouldn't she say it that day, she said it before? Maybe another sister talked about teaching Aboriginal studies, maybe big sister talked about how her Koori-ness framed her contemporary Koori art practice. I might have mentioned the time husband got his gudgegongs mixed up with his gungles. We talked about being Koori, at least our way of being. He says what about me? We look at him. Because I am the bitter one, I say, well, if you would have contributed anything of value you might be included. No-one else says anything and we go back to playing cards.

Hey Trav

A little cone, a little toke, a little needle, a little fucking life,
just say no dickhead,
please
You got stung and marked us all,
a little, a little at a time.
Fifteen years'll do it.
Your voice gone, with the song.

After Cardboard Incarceration

If prisons were cardboard we wouldn't be there in crowds,
If prisons were cardboard, we'd all be escapees,
If escapees wouldn't look to escape, we wouldn't be in prisons in crowds,
If escapees wouldn't look to escape, we wouldn't be recidivists,
If recidivists could see outside themselves, they could live outside.

Mum all over

A murrimul like any other, but different
Capable, line free and big.
Harvesting oysters.
Banging the lime to scar the earth.

Thunna, mundowie slow and jerook,
taking up her share of the earth.
Dancing the pippies up.
Walking the miles to work.

Thumarng, not shapely but passed on.
Where I got my flat arse.

Quandongs

They meet up. They just do. Then they walk over Ngiyaampaa Country, feeling the stones underfoot. Sometimes singly, sometimes spread wide, sometimes in pairs or groups they make their way past mine shafts and rusted out mining equipment; past tumbleweeds waiting for a breeze. The days are long though they have to be home before dark. They aren't to drink the mineral water that lies in an overflow dam near the mine. They have to watch out for the littlies.

The big boys think they are the leaders and take the front rows. The younger boys and then the little kids and then the girls. The girls tend to walk 2, 3, 4, 5 abreast. One day, the big boys laugh and fart to annoy the younger boys and make them swear. The younger boys try to learn how to fart when they want. Little Kev shits his pants he tries so hard. The big girls clean him up because the big boys and the younger boys are too delicate to do it.

They walk through the scrub each carrying a handy stick. They call everything and everyone a bitch, their favourite swear word. Bitch is the word that one mother won't have any child of hers saying. The children say it and they get a flogging and if they don't stop crying there's more where that came from. How do you like that my girl, my boy? Don't look at me like that, I know what that means so just get that look off your face.

The roaming children use their bitch sticks to stick down the trapdoor spider's holes. The bitch spiders try to get out and the children see their long legs emerge from the hole. Jabbing and shrieking. Everyone knows that those bitches jump. The children walk on through tracks that only they know. They talk and laugh but when the girls want a swim everyone heads to a dam. The best dams don't have a dead cow in them. Though that one near the big bushes has leeches so they stay away from that. That one near the old mine has snakes but they are only water snakes and they won't come near the children with all their splashing and kicking.

The group dries off and walk up to the old mine. There is a deep something or other that was part of the mine that fills up with water and frogs which means tadpoles. Sometimes someone has brought a jar, or there has been a jar left there waiting for a return visit and tadpoleing. The big boys climb down with the helping hands and arms of the bigger younger boys and the big girls. The holders lie on the baked bricks holding until the big boys figure out which slots in the brickwork will hold them. When the number of tadpoles in the jar satisfies the big boys the walkers head across to the soft slag hill where they can roll or run down. At the other end of the slag dump is a good birds-nesting site. The big boys and girls climb if they spy a nest. If an egg is found it is exclaimed over by everyone. The lovely colours are remarked on; some wonder if the colours stay the same when the eggs are boiled; some want to take it home and wrap it in clothes and put it under the bed to see if it will grow a bird. A big boy shows his manliness by throwing the egg against a rock. It hurts everyone and he is the biggest bitch of all the bitches, and he should have some mother bird peck his bitch eyes out. There's nothing else left.

They head home. They go via the quandong tree. When they have eaten as much as they can the nuts are collected to be used for conkers or wars out on the flat.

Andraya Stapp-Gaunt

Rabbit-Girl

I crouch before my rabbit
and our noses connect
I sense his lagomorph breath
Beat rapid
He is the prey animal
But I am on my knees
We are alone
Veiled in liminal light
Before the others wake
Before the opening and closing of doors
And mouths
And cereal packets
No one knows our secret
And I, becoming rabbit-girl
Can share my dreams
Beyond the confines of this life
Of running at his side.

George Villaflor

My country is here

I saw
A scarred tree
Ngunnawal Country.
It is not
My country
But I felt good
Tree is young
By tree age
Bark removed
Old
Beyond time
Human hands
Ancient
Human hands
Tree

Looked after the scar
The two
Each other
Against all odds
The tree
Is still alive
Scar
Still sings out
Ancient stories
Ancient people
Touching it
Others
Now watching
The earth
Needs both
We
Are the Earth
Country
Can give
People take
But
Not too greedy
People
Once lived here
People
Still do.
The tree
Is still alive
Message
Is still alive

George Villaflor

This is not my country
Seeing that tree
I felt
Real good.
When I get back
My Country
I will ask
Where is our trees
I hope
There will be
Many.

The leader

He spoke loud and strong
The audience was restless
Someone ordered a coke.

Adaption

An old story
Modern tongue
Different sound
Same meaning.

Goodbyes

Goodbyes are hard
Final ones worst.

Hope

It was here
It is gone
It must be somewhere.

Satisfaction

Refreshing rain
The sun came out
Its hot.

Culture

Ancient peoples
Cameras clicking
The bus pulled up.

Notes on Contributors

EMMA ADAMS is a psychiatrist based in Canberra and is of Wiradjuri descent. Her memoir *Unbreakable Threads: the true story of an Australian mother, a refugee boy and what family really means*, was published in 2018 by Allen & Unwin.

WAYNE APPLEBEE, 71, is a Kamilaroi elder currently completing a PhD titled *From Homo Sacer to Subaltern: Becoming Aboriginal Online*. Wayne commenced study late – aged 57 he commenced a law degree only to realize re-education of the colonists is the only way to change Aboriginals' circumstances. "The Wayback Machine" is part of re-educating the future – from our horrid past.

KRIS BEATTIE is a Noongar man from Perth, south of the Swan River which is located in the south-west of Western Australia. Although born on Warjak boudja (Perth) he spent the first 10 years of his childhood raised on country. On his 10th birthday he relocated to the eastern states of Australia with his mother and younger sister. Leaving Noongar boudja left him broken-hearted and in despair as his connection to country every day seemed to drift further into distance. He is currently living in Canberra attending one of the local universities studying a Bachelor of Science in Psychology and is in his final year of his undergraduate degree with aspirations of being a Clinical Psychologist. Kris is not afraid to admit that reading and writing have always been a challenge him. He said, "All that changed after meeting an Indigenous writer by the name of Paul Collis.... He's the author of *Dancing Home*, a book which has been inspirational and empowering". Paul's mentoring has given Kris the courage to write poetry and to follow in his footsteps as Kris has started writing a novel of his own.

VALERIE M. BICHARD is a multidisciplinary arts practitioner and educator who has published poetry in a number of Pacific anthologies. Her inspiration is drawn from her dynamic family histories and personal experiences in Oceania and Australia. Valerie is currently the Pacific Adviser to the Royal Norwegian Embassy in Canberra.

PAUL COLLIS is a Barkindji person from Bourke, on the Darling River in north-west New South Wales. His novel *Dancing Home* was the winner of the 2016 David Unaipon Award, and was published in 2017 by the University of Queensland Press. He teaches creative writing at the University of Canberra, where he earned a PhD in Communications.

ELLIOT COOPER is a freelance academic, treehugger and neo-troglodyte mountain goat. His 2015 PhD is an intellectual excavation which uncovers origins of key psychological concepts of Saussurean general linguistics in Flournoitian cryptomnesia and Sanskritoid teleological automatism performed by the spiritualist Elise Muller.

JEN CRAWFORD is Assistant Professor of Writing at the University of Canberra. She has had the pleasure of working with Paul Collis on the Story Ground Project as funded by the Indigenous Languages and Arts Program since 2017, and collaborating together on teaching and pedagogy for a couple of years before that. Learning about Culture and Country is a daily renewal.

DENNIS FOLEY is Gai-mariagal from northern Sydney, a Cammeraigal man, his father is Wiradjuri of the Turon River clans. His inaugural text, *Repossession of our Spirits* (Aboriginal History) achieved wide acclaim. He has consistently published poetry in eclectic mediums including *Meanjin* and various Indigenous Journals. He has a PhD in Indigenous Entrepreneurship and teaches the same at the University of Canberra.

CHELLA GOLDWIN is a Meriam Kosker a descendant from Erub Island in the Torres Strait. She has written works in the anthology *Too Deadly* published by the ACT Us Mob Writing Corporation. She is passionate about her content which largely focuses on her family history, Australian colonisation with her cultural and spiritual insights. She writes with message to inform the reader of life as an Torres Strait Islander woman and Indigenous Australian.

TJANARA GORENG GORENG is a Wakka Wakka Wulli Wulli cultural teacher, academic, writer and published poet. Tjanara's memoir *A Long Way from No Go* was published by Wild Dingo Press in 2017 and she began Deadly

Dingo Books as an Imprint of Wild Dingo Press to support mid career First Nations poets to publish their poetry. Tjanara's poetry is published in *Inside Black Australia*, edited by Kevin Gilbert, and she is a member of the ACT Us Mob Writers Group.

BECCA GOSCH is a Birripai Woman who grew up in Alice Springs, with feet that yearn for sparkling red sand, and that turn her towards the Ocean, her own true north. She is a student at the University of Canberra studying Culture and Heritage as well as Creative Writing. She lives in Canberra with her cat (Mirrah) who rescued her from Uni one day, and in her free time she runs her own Karate Dojo where she teaches kids and adults a tradtitional form of the Martial Art.

NYINGARI LITTLE is a student of Secondary Education majoring in English and Indigenous Studies at the University of Canberra. She was the 2017 NAIDOC Scholar of the Year and was awarded a 2019 Aboriginal and Torres Strait Islander Tertiary Scholarship.

AZLAN MARTIN is an emerging Nunga poet and creative who writes narrative stories of place, and the connections that bind us. Azlan was born and grown on boodja (Western Australia) and is currently studying postgraduate counselling in Melbourne. She appeared at the 2019 Emerging Writer's Festival and is currently working on her first collection of poetry and prose.

HANGAMA OBAIDULLA came to Australia from Afghanistan as a refugee in August 2003. At that time she spoke no English, but in October that year she began her English language studies and rapidly completed 500 hours. She enrolled as a mature age student at St Mary's Senior High School, Sydney, NSW, graduating with her Higher School Certificate in 2009. Since arriving in Australia, Hangama has developed her arts practice in painting, drawing, photography and writing. She moved to Canberra in 2010 where she is currently studying for a Bachelor of Writing at University of Canberra. She has regularly participated in a variety of conferences and events for women and refugees. Hangama's work draws on her Afghan heritage, her homeland and its history. Her goal is to assist other Afghan women and children though her visual arts practice and her writing.

ROSITA RANDLE is an English teacher with a background in law. She came to Canberra from Byron bay and Brisbane for a career change and found an unexpected connection to Ngunnawal country through the gum trees.

WENDY SOMERVILLE is a salt-water Jerrinja woman of the South Coast of NSW who was born on red-earth Ngiyampaa Country in north west NSW. She is writing a PhD and is employed as a teaching fellow at the University of Canberra.

ANDRAYA STAPP-GAUNT was born in New Zealand but has spent most of her life in South Australia and the ACT. She loves animals and prefers quiet time in the company of her four house rabbits who teach her many things. Andi is currently enrolled in a PhD in writing at the University of Canberra and is an English teacher with the ACT ED.

GEORGE VILLAFLOR is a Wagiman man from the Northern Territory. He has been involved in Indigenous issues since the early 80's and was once Editor of *The North Queensland Land Council's at Cairns*, a land rights publication which sparked his interest in writing. He became a lawyer and barrister and is currently writing to eventually publish about the years of the "Aboriginal struggles" that he was involved in. He currently lives at Canberra.

www.ingramcontent.com/pod-product-compliance
Lightning Source LLC
Chambersburg PA
CBHW020330010526
44107CB00054B/2052